S0-FBV-071

MY FIRST READING BOOK

Questron®

PRICE STERN SLOAN

Los Angeles

THE QUESTRON® SYSTEM
COMBINING FUN WITH LEARNING

This book is part of **THE QUESTRON SYSTEM**, which offers children a unique aid to learning and endless hours of challenging entertainment.

The QUESTRON electronic "wand" uses a microchip to sense correct and incorrect answers with "right" or "wrong" sounds and lights. Victory sounds and lights reward the user when particular sets of questions or games are completed. Powered by a nine-volt alkaline battery, which is activated only when the wand is pressed on a page, QUESTRON should have an exceptionally long life. The QUESTRON ELECTRONIC WAND can be used with any book in the QUESTRON series.

A note to parents...

With QUESTRON, right or wrong answers are indicated instantly and can be tried over and over to reinforce learning and improve skills. Children need not be restricted to the books designated for their age group, as interests and rates of development vary widely. Also, within many of the books, certain pages are designed for the older end of the age group and will provide a stimulating challenge to younger children.

Many activities are designed at different levels. For example, the child can select an answer by recognizing a letter or by reading an entire word. The activities for pre-readers and early readers are intended to be used with parental assistance. Interaction with parents or older children will stimulate the learning experience.

QUESTRON Project Director: Roger Burrows
Educational Consultants: Rozanne Lanczak, Susan Parker
Writer: Beverley Dietz
Illustrator: Klaus Björkman
Graphic Designers: Judy Walker, Lee A. Scott

ISBN: 0-8431-3107-1
4 5 6 7 8 9 0

HOW TO START QUESTRON

Hold **QUESTRON**
at this angle and
press the activator button
firmly on the page.

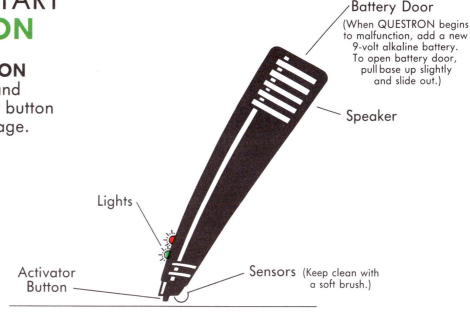

Battery Door
(When QUESTRON begins
to malfunction, add a new
9-volt alkaline battery.
To open battery door,
pull base up slightly
and slide out.)

Speaker

Lights

Activator
Button

Sensors (Keep clean with
a soft brush.)

HOW TO USE QUESTRON

PRESS
Press **QUESTRON** firmly
on the shape below,
then lift it off.

TRACK
Press **QUESTRON** down on "Start"
and keep it pressed down
as you move to "Finish."

Start   Finish

RIGHT & WRONG WITH QUESTRON

Press **QUESTRON**
on the square.

See the green light and
hear the sound. This
green light and sound
say "You are correct."

Press **QUESTRON**
on the triangle.

The red light and sound
say "Try again." Lift
QUESTRON off the page and
wait for the sound to stop.

Press **QUESTRON**
on the circle.

Hear the victory sound.
Don't be dazzled
by the flashing lights.
You deserve them.

Animal Search

Track **Questron** on the path that has the pictures that match the words. Start on the ★.

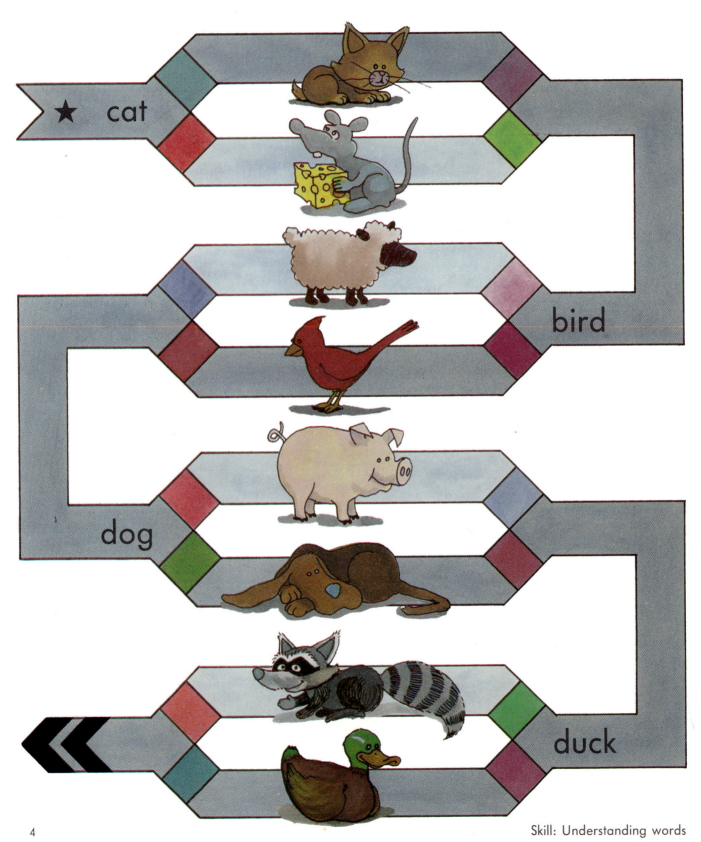

★ cat

bird

dog

duck

Skill: Understanding words

Friends and Neighbors

Track **Questron** on the path that has the words that match the pictures. Start on the ★.

farmer

baker

doctor

boy

king

girl

man

woman

In Action

Read the sentence. Press **Questron** on the box in the picture that matches the sentence.

The pigs run.

The bear sleeps.

The cat walks.

The boy smiles.

The dog eats.

Skill: Understanding sentences

The frog jumps.

The girl talks.

The birds fly.

The fish swims.

The rabbit hops.

Day and Night

Look at the pictures. Press **Questron** on the sentences that match the pictures.

The hill is on the house.	The bird is in the tree.
The house is on the hill.	The tree is in the bird.
The flower is on the bee.	The sun is in the sky.
The bee is on the flower.	The sky is in the sun.

Skill: Understanding sentences

The moon shines at night.

A car barks at the dog.

The night shines at moon.

A dog barks at the car.

A hill goes down the car.

Two stars are in the sky.

A car goes down the hill.

The sky is in two stars.

Up, Up and Away

Look at the balloons. Track **Questron** to the word that finishes each sentence best. Start on the ★.

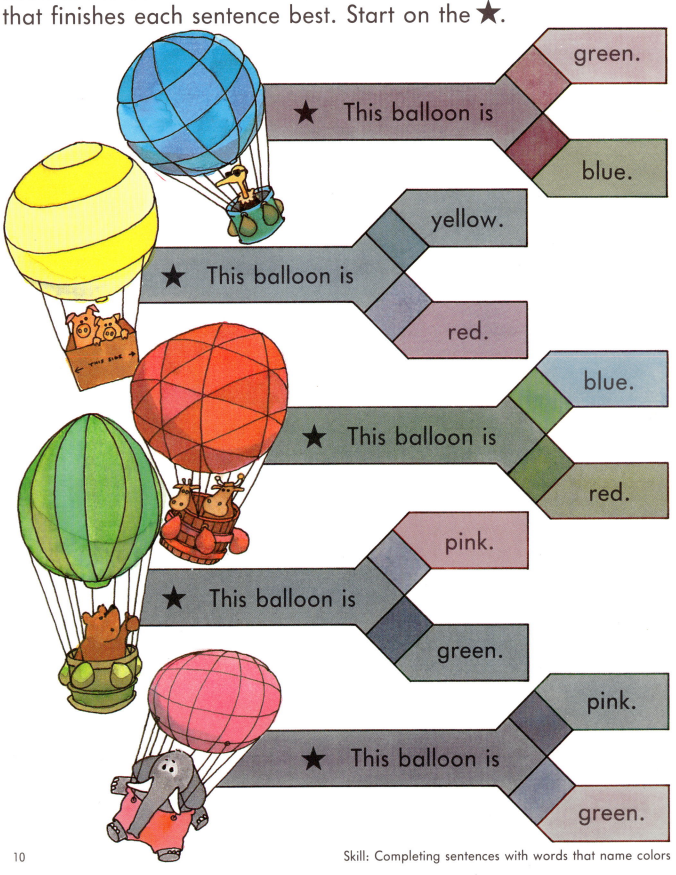

★ This balloon is — green. / blue.

★ This balloon is — yellow. / red.

★ This balloon is — blue. / red.

★ This balloon is — pink. / green.

★ This balloon is — pink. / green.

Skill: Completing sentences with words that name colors

Where's the Bug?

Look at each picture. Press **Questron** on the word that finishes each sentence best.

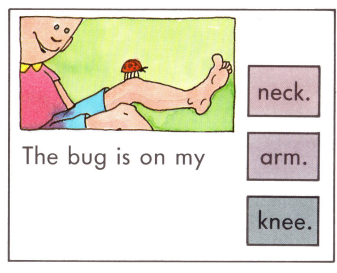

The bug is on my

neck.

arm.

knee.

The bug is on my

arm.

ear.

leg.

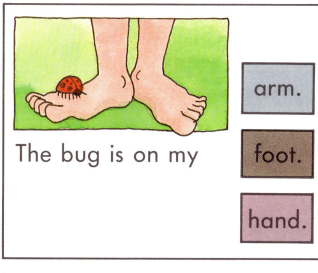

The bug is on my

arm.

foot.

hand.

The bug is on my

knee.

lips.

head.

The bug is on my

hand.

leg.

ear.

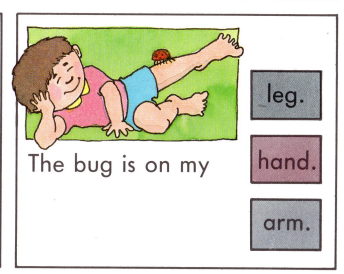

The bug is on my

leg.

hand.

arm.

At the Store

Which sentences make sense?
Press **Questron** on those sentences.

Likes the Terry bananas yellow.	Apples red Jim some wants.
Terry likes the yellow bananas.	Jim wants some red apples.
Girls ice cream some two want.	Ann sees the corn.
Two girls want some ice cream.	Corn the sees Ann.

Skill: Recognizing natural word order and understanding sentences

Three boys look at the cakes.

At cakes three look the boys.

The children pay for the food.

The food for children the pay.

The children go to the store.

Children the store to go the.

Sam and Sue buy some eggs.

Sue and eggs buy some Sam.

Riddles

Read each riddle. Press **Questron** on the box inside the picture that answers the riddle best.

I have four legs
and a tail.

I can roar.

You can see me in
the zoo.

What am I?

I am orange.

You cut a face
in me.

You put a light
inside me.

What am I?

I have many keys.

They are black
and white.

You can make
music on me.

What am I?

Skill: Understanding sentences and solving riddles

Read each riddle. Press **Questron** on the box inside the picture that answers the riddle best.

I have four legs.
I cannot walk.
You can sit on me.
What am I?

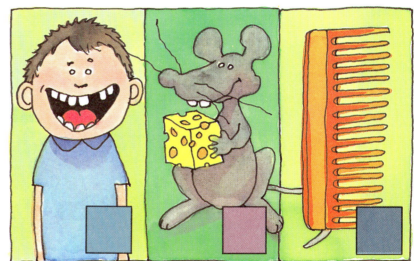

I have teeth.
I cannot eat.
You use me on your hair.
What am I?

I have a long string.
I have a tail.
You can fly me in the wind.
What am I?

Skill: Understanding sentences and solving riddles

Around the Farm

Read the directions. Track **Questron** on the correct path. Start on the ★.

Go through the gate.
Go into the field.
Go past the cows.
Go over the bridge.
Go between the pigs
and past the horses.
Then go into the barn.

Skill: Understanding and following directions

Nursery Rhyme Time

Look at each picture. Track **Questron** to the words that finish the sentence best. Start on the ★.

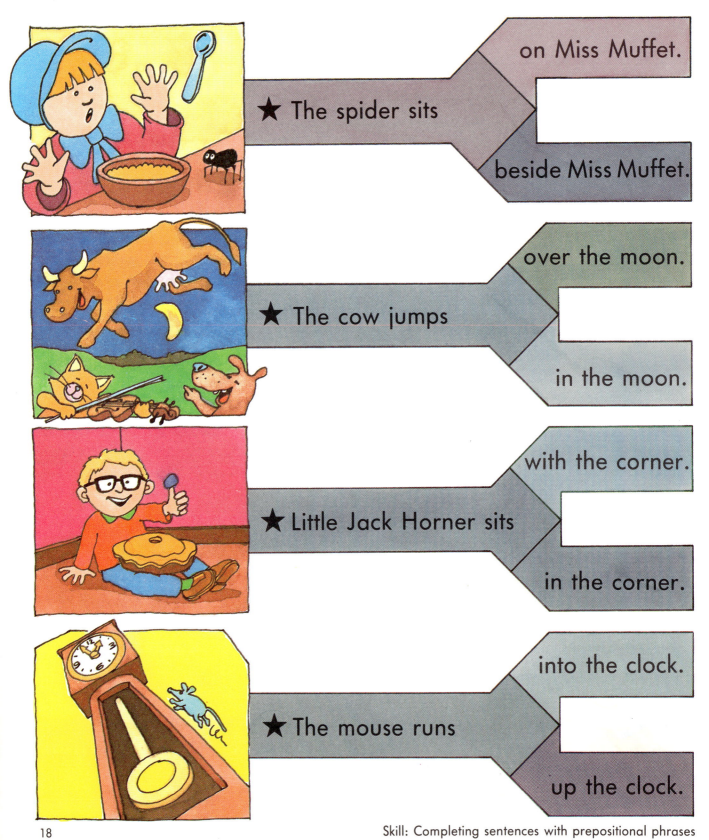

★ The spider sits

on Miss Muffet.

beside Miss Muffet.

★ The cow jumps

over the moon.

in the moon.

★ Little Jack Horner sits

with the corner.

in the corner.

★ The mouse runs

into the clock.

up the clock.

Skill: Completing sentences with prepositional phrases

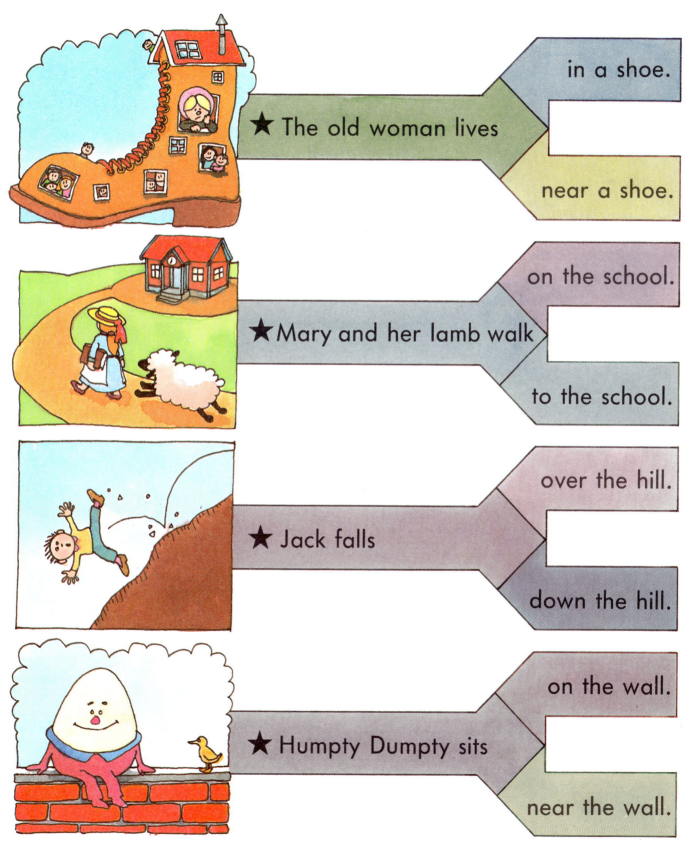

★ The old woman lives

in a shoe.

near a shoe.

★ Mary and her lamb walk

on the school.

to the school.

★ Jack falls

over the hill.

down the hill.

★ Humpty Dumpty sits

on the wall.

near the wall.

Monkey Business

Which words make a sentence about each picture?
Track **Questron** on those words. Start on the ★.

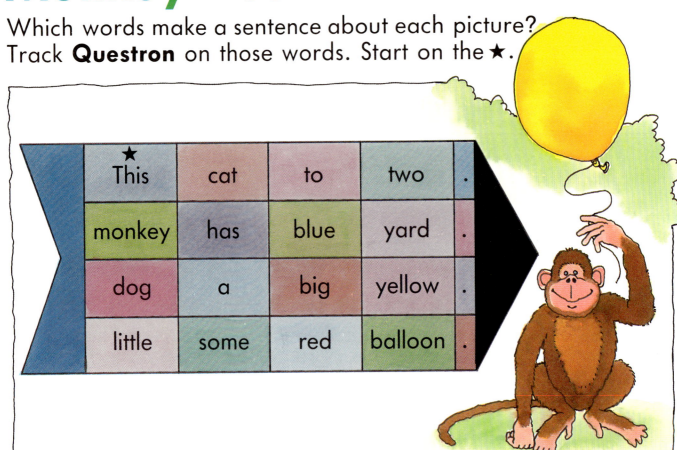

★ This	cat	to	two	.
monkey	has	blue	yard	.
dog	a	big	yellow	.
little	some	red	balloon	.

★ This	monkey	in	for	.
rabbit	is	it	from	.
goes	standing	on	foot	.
with	looks	his	head	.

Skill: Understanding and composing statements

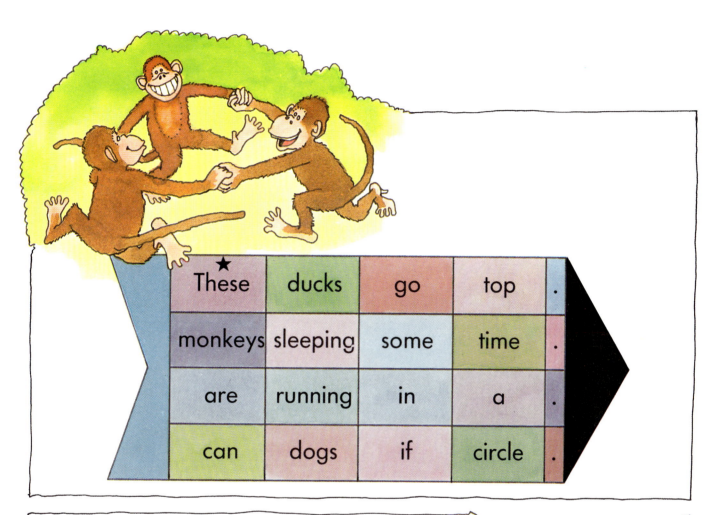

★ These	ducks	go	top	.
monkeys	sleeping	some	time	.
are	running	in	a	.
can	dogs	if	circle	.

★ This	monkey	is	in	.
money	friend	hanging	by	.
move	farm	hoping	his	.
make	frog	with	tail	.

Monster Magic

Read each question. Press **Questron** on
the picture that answers the question best.

Which monster
is Morton?

Morton has four
dogs. Which dog
is the biggest?

Morton has three
cats. Which cat
is the smallest?

Morton has three
pet snakes.
Which snake is
the longest?

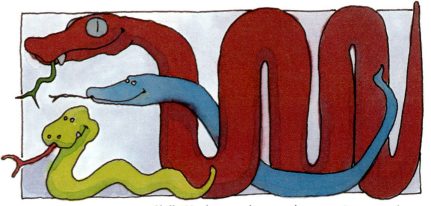

Skill: Understanding and answering questions

Morton sees four trees. Which tree is the highest?

Morton has three friends. Which friend is the happiest?

Morton sees three buildings. Which building is the shortest?

Morton sees four clouds. Which cloud is the darkest?

Elephant Jokes

Track **Questron** on the words that make a question about each picture.

★Why	what	tag	try	?
is	if	tug	trip	?
this	then	time	trap	?
elephant	in	a	tree	?

Answer: To make a monkey out of himself.

★What	does	the	then	?
eight	egg	elephant	easy	?
car	took	ask	the	?
where	who	boy	bird	?

Answer: "Mommy?"

Skill: Understanding and composing questions

★ Why	that	walk	yellow	?
does	this	with	green	?
door	elephant	wear	blue	?
when	where	shop	shoes	?

Answer: His red shoes are wet.

★ Why	does	same	eleven	?
can	this	find	elephant	?
cat	elephant	too	sky	?
cup	fly	in	the	?

Answer: His feet hurt!

Whatever the Weather

Read each question.
Press **Questron** on the best answer.

Why does Wilma have a broom?

She is going to brush her teeth.

She is going to sweep the floor.

She is going to draw a picture.

Why does Wilma have a shovel?

She is going to feed the birds.

She is going to watch television.

She is going to dig in the garden.

Why does Wilma have a pen
and some paper?

She is going to write a letter.

She is going to bake a cake.

She is going to clean her room.

Skill: Understanding and answering cause-and-effect questions

Why does Wilma have a
big paintbrush?

She is going to water the flowers.

She is going to paint the fence.

She is going to wash her hands.

Why does Wilma have a rake?

She is going to work in the garden.

She is going to read a story.

She is going to feed the goldfish.

Why does Wilma have a leash?

She is going to set the table.

She is going to feed the cat.

She is going to walk the dog.

Animal Fun

Read about each animal. Which picture shows that animal? Press **Questron** on the box in that picture.

Curlie Cow is very pretty. She is brown and white. She wears a red ribbon on her head. She smiles and waves her long tail.

Danny Dragon is big and mean. He has sharp teeth. He has a long tail. It has a point at the end. Danny is green all over.

28

Skill: Understanding descriptive paragraphs

Boris Bug is very friendly. He smiles and waves at everyone. Boris has a black body. He has bright red wings.

Katie Cat is big and fluffy. She is gray with one white spot. She wears a blue ribbon around her neck. A little bell hangs from the ribbon.

Shopping Trips

Read each story. Which picture shows what will happen next? Press **Questron** on the box in that picture.

Zeke and his mother go to the store. They buy some wood. They buy a hammer and some nails, too. Then they take everything home. What will happen next?

Jane and her father go to the pet store. Jane likes a little dog most of all. She pets the little dog. The little dog wags its tail. Jane's father smiles. He talks to the lady in the store. What will happen next?

Skill: Understanding stories and predicting outcomes

Mark and Molly go to the store. They find a loaf of bread. Mark gets some butter. Molly gets some jam. They pay for the food. Then they take the food home. What will happen next?

Tina and her grandmother go to the store. They buy a big box of paints. They buy two paintbrushes. They also buy some paper. Tina and her grandmother take everything home. What will happen next?

THE QUESTRON LIBRARY OF ELECTRONIC BOOKS

A series of books specially designed to
reach—and teach—and entertain children of all ages

QUESTRON ELECTRONIC WORKBOOKS

Early Childhood

My First Counting Book	Reading Readiness
My First ABC Book	My First Words
My First Book of Animals	My First Numbers
Shapes and Sizes	Going Places
Preschool Skills	Kindergarten Skills
My First Vocabulary	Sesame Street® 1 to 10
My First Nursery Rhymes	Sesame Street® A to Z

Autos, Ships, Trains and Planes

Grades K–5

My First Reading Book (K–1)
Little Miss™ — First School Days (K–2)
Mr. Men™ — A First Reading Adventure (K–2)
Word Games (K–2)
My First Book of Telling Time (K–2)
Day of the Dinosaur (K–3)
First Grade Skills (1)
My First Book of Addition (1–2)
Bigger, Smaller, Shorter, Taller... (1–3)
The Storytime Activity Book (1–3)
My Robot Book (1–3)
My First Book of Spelling (1–3)
My First Book of Subtraction (1–3)
My First Book of Multiplication (2–3)
I Want to Be... (2–5)
Number Fun (2–5)
Word Fun (2–5)

Electronic Quizbooks for the Whole Family

Trivia Fun and Games
How, Why, Where and When
More How, Why, Where and When
World Records and Amazing Facts

The Princeton Review S.A.T.® Program

The Princeton Review: S.A.T.® Math
The Princeton Review: S.A.T.® Verbal

PRICE STERN SLOAN
Los Angeles